# Pastoring from a Biblical View

# PASTORING FROM A BIBLICAL VIEW

by

Dr. Gilbert Noah Burkett

**DORRANCE PUBLISHING CO., INC.**
**PITTSBURGH, PENNSYLVANIA 15222**

ISBN # 0-8059-6812-1
Printed in the United States of America

First Printing

For information or to order additional books, please write:
Dorrance Publishing Co., Inc.
701 Smithfield Street
Third Floor
Pittsburgh, Pennsylvania 15222
U.S.A.
1-800-788-7654
Or visit our website and on-line catalog at
www.dorrancepublishing.com

# Dedication

In remembrance of my father, The Reverend William Noah Burkett, whose godly influence, friendship, and love still encourages me today to give of my best to the Master. I appreciate his dedicated and patient service in pastoral ministry over a period of many years throughout the state of Michigan.

To my mother, Myrtle Fisher Burkett-Ross, for her tireless service and faithful witness to the power of our Lord Jesus Christ, who laid the spiritual foundation in my life, I dedicate this writing.

# Contents

# Acknowledgements

The inestimable value of a praying church, such is St. Marks Baptist Church. You have been the motivator behind getting this work done. I thank you, Church family, for your commitment to my serving you these thirty-four years as your Senior Pastor.

My deepest appreciation to my wife and companion, Phyllis, whose editing and word processing of this material onto computer disc assisted greatly in getting the work ready for printing.

My special thanks and appreciation to my friend and colleague in ministry, Dr. Eugene Hudson, Pastor of Rocky Mount Missionary Baptist Church, located in New York City. I'm thankful, "Hud" for the many years you served so well as my assistant. Also, thank you for allowing me to reap extensive blessings teaching at the Rocky Mount Bible Institute.

Much thanks to the Metropolitan Minister's Interdenominational Conference, under the leader ship of the spiritually gifted and humble servant, Reverend Dr. Thomas E. Moore—your interest and encouragement in this project is greatly appreciated.

To my ten siblings, who've been my inspiration throughout my Christian life: Horace, Robert, Charles, Bernadine, Wilbert, Willie Ann (Babe), Uriel, Drusilla, Evvie T, and Leon. Thank you, family.

To my son by birth and in ministry, Vincent Burkett, thank you for your encouragement and genuine interest in my work. Thanks for your expressions of love to your "Pop," especially when illness came to call.

Special thanks to my other children: Wanda, Pamela, Vanessa, Eric, and Craig.

Above all, I am most grateful to my Lord and Savior Jesus Christ, our soon-coming King. I thank Him for giving me the strength and fortitude to pursue this task. My prayer is that this pleases Him and that many people will be blessed by it.

# Introduction

The Christian ministry seems to be on a downward spiral. This is due mainly to the overwhelming amount of hypocrisy that has crept within the ministerial ranks. Satan has infiltrated the ministry with many unsaved people who facilitate the idea that holiness is humanly unattainable; therefore, pursuing it is discouraged. We are grateful that there are still remaining those whom God has called and ordained to this great task who have not succumbed to carnality. That is why it is imperative that the minister be dedicated to the Lord in order to do God-pleasing service that will meet His approval.

The Christian ministry is the greatest vocation in the entire world. The president of the United States' task cannot be equated with that of the Gospel minister. The President's concerns are focused on material aspects, while, on the other hand, the minister of the Lord is not only ministering to the physical realm, but also has as his primary function to lead men to Christ. He is employed in the business of shaping the immortal destiny of the soul according to the Word of God. This great responsibility that has been placed on the minister's shoulders, is the most strenuous profession that can be entrusted to an individual. Yet, it also carries with it happiness, joy, and satisfaction, in the knowledge that lost souls are being ushered into the kingdom of God.

In our scientific space-age where atheism and skepticism abounds, the Christian Minister must be bold as a lion, standing with "loins girt about with truth, and feet shod with the preparation of the gospel of peace. And having done all, to stand!" (Eph. 6:13-15).

There is a tremendous need to increase the ranks of preachers who take their work seriously. There is an imminent need to equip those who preach with the resources of an instructional aptitude, so that he can minister without the overwhelming stress or emotional drainage that often occur because of inadequate preparation.

The only genuine source of instruction on pastoral ministry is the Holy Bible. It is the power of God's presence, in the person of the Holy Spirit, that enables ministers and servants to wisely impart these Biblical instructions. The ministry of extending grace to hurting and broken people, feeding the new convert, strengthening growing believers, and cultivating a congregation so that it is producing spiritual fruit is the objective and purpose of knowing how to administer pastoral care.

Ingersoll, an agnostic of expansive influence, challengingly sneered that if he believed as Christians do regarding the Bible's view on hell, he would run through glass shoeless, warning men to flee from such a place. Since we know God's Word is true and we have the privilege to look into such a place for just one second and to view those souls there in their agony, we would be less timid in our proclamation of the gospel. Because the hour is fast approaching, daily, we unwaveringly agree with the prophet Jeremiah as he spoke this warning to Israel by saying, "The harvest is past, the summer is ended, and we are not saved." As men of God, we must not fail to warn the people; their blood will be required at our hands.

The minister has the most potent agencies within his disposal—God the Father, God the Son, and God the Holy Ghost—to comfort, guide, direct, and keep the man of God. He has given us the assurance in the Gospel recorded by Matthew, that He would never leave us, nor forsake us, but that He would be with us always, even until the end of the world (Matt. 28:20). God's precious Word is the preacher's authority. In his moments of despondency, it is his source of strength, courage, and comfort.

The preacher is under divine obligation to herald the Gospel of the grace of God to all men:

Teaching them that denying all ungodliness and worldly lusts, they should live soberly and righteously and godly in this present world, looking for that blessed hope and glorious appearing of the Great god and our Savior Jesus Christ; Who gave Himself to redeem mankind from all iniquity and purifying unto Himself to redeem a peculiar people zealous of good works (Titus 2:11-14).

There is no room for hatred and prejudiced in this magnificent profession, regardless of race, color, creed, or ethnic background; no matter how great or small "every knee must bow to the Lord, and every tongue shall confess to God" (Rom. 14:11).

When we appear at the "Bema," or "Judgment Seat of Christ," we will be rewarded according to how we have carried out our divine entrustment.

Our Lord has given us several offices for the edification of the body of Christ, working together in harmony.

And He gave some, apostles; and some, prophets; and some, evangelists; and some, pastors and teachers; for the work of the ministry, for the edifying of the body of Christ: Till we all come into the unity of the faith, and of the knowledge of the son of God unto a perfect man, unto the measure of the stature of the fullness of Christ: that we henceforth be no more tossed to and fro, and carried about with every wind of doctrine by the sleight of men, and cunning craftiness, whereby they lie in wait to deceive; But speaking the truth in love may grow up into Him in all things which is the head even Christ: From whom the whole body fitly joined together and compacted by that which every joint supplieth, according to the effectual working in the measure of every part, maketh increase of the body unto the edifying of itself in love (Eph. 4:11-16).

My humblest prayer is that whoever will have access to this dissertation will find it a source of interest, the pastoral ministry greatly magnified, and the ethics set forth in this work will be a unifying factor in contributing glory and honor to our Triune God.

Gilbert N. Burkett
Brooklyn, New York
January 25, 2003

# CHAPTER ONE

## The Christian Minister

What is this area of Christian ministry referred to as pastoral theology? As often as this topic comes under discussion, it still remains a difficult category of ministry to astutely define. The most probable description is to attach it to the responsibility of the teaching, preaching, and shepherding ministry of the pastor. Our Savior has left explicit and various instruments for us to bring the unsaved into the kingdom of God. Witnessing, intercessory praying, and sharing of goods are many avenues we may use to reach and reach out to others for Christ, but the Christian ministry is the one area most utilized of those He has provided.

1. Superior in Calling: Every born-again minister humbly admits that his calling into Christ's ministry is one that is divine in origin, and superior to any call or commitment he has ever received and answered. However, not all are called to become pastors; yet, all are called to service. Specifically, the call to pastoral ministry revolves around the spiritual attributes, or gifts, bequeathed to one who is destined to shepherd the flock. Thomas C. Ogden has defined this by stating, "Pastoral theology is that branch of Christian theology that

deals with the office, gifts, and functions of the pastor. As theology, pastoral theology seeks to reflect upon that self-disclosure of God witnessed to in Scripture, mediated through tradition, reflected upon by critical reasoning, and embodied in personal and social experience" (Pastoral Theology, 311).[1]

The background for pastoral service will be linked to the Biblical record as early as Moses' trek through the wilderness, leading the multitude from Egyptian bondage, until he brings them face to face with the new land of promise (Exod. 12–Deut. 33). The $23^{rd}$ Psalm, the most recited verses in the Bible, captures our minds with the impressive first line, "the Lord is my Shepherd." This is lucid in its indication that the shepherding ministry is primary in the heart of God. This tenderly defined relationship indicates a relationship of care and compassion—of selflessness and guardianship that is representative in the title and responsibility accompanying the vocation.

Jeremiah's unique call informs us that a divine call can be initiated on a man's life as early as before the embryo forms in the womb. This setting aside for divine service is clearly and distinctly evidenced as the life of the individual develops and his heart responds to the conviction of the Holy Spirit. This call is superior to any goals or objectives a believer may direct his attention. Nothing provides any satisfaction in return or reward until submission to this call. God will not be denied, and any servant willingly yielded will never be disappointed with God's offer of companionship in the labor. The resulting reward of a fruitful life lived in partnership with the Lord will be a legacy of fruitful lives left to carrying on the work of making disciples. Men, women, boys, and girls whose lives have been transformed will expand the life and work of such a committed servant. Revelation informs us in chapter 14, verse 13: "Blessed are the dead who die in the Lord from henceforth. Yea, saith the Spirit the Spirit, that they may rest from their labors; and their works do follow them."

We can never minimize the importance of faithfulness in the life of the Christian minister. The tasks we face can be and often are daunting and discouraging, but we are to apply ourselves to the life of dependency on the Great Shepherd while remaining faithful to the tasks that confront us. The superiority of the call is noteworthy in that it requires us to be faithful unto the point of death (Rev. 2:10).

It is essential that we extrapolate the meaning of "call" and not so much attach it to the minister and his work, as to completely connect the call to the one who has issued it. The Lord God is the magnet to which we, the servants, are drawn. The call is for His glory as well as the service rendered is for His glory. The significance is that the Omnipotent God has desired to use a specific individual for His glorious service. This places the request to usefulness in a different category; it is a journey for which it is impossible to anticipate its daily encounters or pre-plan the effectiveness of its events. However, those willing to stand true in their "calling" will find their efforts fruitful and the precious Word of God honored in the lives of those being led.

2. <u>Superior in Deportment:</u> Those in the Christian ministry, no matter how challenging or discouraging the tasks become, must not fail to display a mark of superiority in our deportment. Our integrity must not be compromised morally or spiritually. We are stage-setters for that which God has manifested in His Word as "epistles" read by all men. Whether we like it or not, we are targets of sharp criticism from those outside the ministerial profession, and even sharper criticism from those within. It is imperative that the minister, by his deed in public and private, hold high the established reputation of the Christian ministry, without becoming pharisaic about others faults, because the inner voice constantly reminds us that we are all targets of temptation. Nevertheless, our conduct is our human behavior, but the Christian faith has as its undergirding the hidden springs of action, motives, desires, and inspiration. This conduct is also behavior selected and directed by a person in the light of principles or characteristics higher than what is humanly acceptable. Our acting and interacting is to treat the principles of our human responses to divine scrutiny. Our thoughts, inner desires, and drives are never hidden from His view. To openly lay our souls bare to God's perusal in confession and repentance is to disarm the Tempter.

With this particular thought in mind, the Christian minister must exert extra care not to act in any manner that will bring dishonor to his calling. Conduct that we observe and agree is unbecoming in a gentleman is always conduct unbecoming in a minister; as ministers must also remember that conduct sometimes not considered unbecoming in others may not be becoming in ministers. The pulpit should be a place of reverence as well as the sanctuary, if not more so. Conduct there should never be used as a stage to exhibit pride, folly, favoritism, or any other traits that are detrimental to the divine calling.

God's man should never lose sight of this inalterable truth: he is being constantly watched by others. His life is to be blameless and without ethical flaw. He is to live in constant awareness that he is an ambassador for Jesus and that the victory he seeks to gain for the kingdom is connected to his deportment as Christ's ambassador. The verse that succinctly sums this up is Matthew's gospel chapter 5, verse 16; it states, "Let your light so shine before men that they may see your good works and glorify your Father which is in heaven."

The very relevant idea that ministers should understand is that there is an accountability factor predetermined in their ministry. Even if they fail to sense the independence that is often felt as leader or shepherd of a congregation, it is really a relationship of interdependence. It exists between congregation and pastor as they are to uphold one another in prayer and in view and review church objectives and finances. It is best carried out if the man of God has a genuine friend who will also hold him accountable in his personal walk. Sun Valley California's Pastor of Grace Community Church, John MacArthur, J., wrote adroitly about the necessity of pervasiveness accountability. He writes:

"He must have an accountability first to God. I love the Lord and I don't want to do what dishonors Him; that is the most intimate aspect of my accountability and the highest point, because that's a twenty-four hour a day relationship through all of life. Next, I have a point of accountability at home with my wife and children. I want to lead them to love God and serve Him, and I don't want to disappoint them or lead them astray. I don't want to lead them to distrust my devotion to Christ, and thereby cheapen their understanding of Christian faith and commitment. Too much is at stake in their lives and the lives of their families. Third, I have personal accountability to men who labor with me and are my friends." (370)[2]

The minister must be ever mindful of the fact that he is being constantly watched by others. His life should be blameless and without flaw. This in no way intimates that he is perfect in righteous, other than in Jesus' righteousness, but rather he realizes that his private life and his public life is the same. He is an ambassador of Christ, and he is to live a life of victory.

As the Apostle Paul had his critics, so will men of God, but the criticism should not have opportunity to be proven true if it is directed towards the spiritual or moral behavior of God's servant. Jesus' Sermon on the Mount, recorded by Matthew, in chapter 5, verse 16, beautifully defines the minister's conduct, "Let your light so shine before men that they may see your good works and glorify your Father which is in heaven."

3. Superior in Service: The service of the Christian minister is judged on its quality rather than its quantity. His service must be geared by a high mark of faithfulness, never losing sight of the fact that he is a steward of the Lord. Whatever he does should be done "heartily unto the Lord and not unto men, knowing that of the Lord ye shall receive the reward of the inheritance, for ye serve the Lord Christ" (Col. 3:23-24).

As a servant, he is called upon to administer to the needs of those not only in the church, but also to his community and to society at large. Therefore, he must guard against a spirit of laziness that will usurp his influence and credibility as a true servant of God. Laziness will lead to compromise his effectiveness in preaching sermons that feed the flock of God, thus inviting disaster and controversy into his ministry. He must not allow himself to become distracted by the many appealing but busy work tasks that prevent him from laboring in the Word. He must guard against those tasks that prevent his efforts of building godly character into his life through diligence—the spiritual, physical, and emotional training we refer to as discipline. His priorities should be so clearly defined that there should be no second guessing about the seriousness of his personal walk, his prayer life, and the intensity he applies to the study of God's Word, so lucid, in that his congregation is knowledgeable of his status as a man of God.

The idea that temptations assail the man of God with a fierce and continual struggle to overcome him should not be taken lightly. It is to our advantage to approach our involvement in this specific field of labor as combat. The enemy, we know, is our own flesh and the

Devil's access to our weaknesses. Feeding on the Word is the only way to pure living; not just occasional reading or deep study of Scripture, but applying what is taught in every verse on moral character and faith produces a pure conscience and walk with God and man. Holiness is a trait God expects in his servants. Unfortunately, we have settled for the idiomatic excuse, "he is only human"; therefore, when an opportunity to give in to evil faces us, we are quick to apply that excuse to ourselves. Sin in the life of a leader assaults him with poor judgment, poor judgment in selecting quality and qualified leaders in our ministry. Rather than seek men of high moral standing, we tend to look for those whose weaknesses are somewhat akin to our own. We shy away from persons with obvious, high spiritual qualities because their righteous mindsets tend to offend us. So we overlook the faithful, the virtuous, and those exuding wise counsel in favor of those whose attitude toward worldliness is more palatable with what is secretly in our hearts. It is essential that a ministry is built on qualities that give evidence that they are in residence in the lives of any leader.

A minister is required to serve and administer to the needs of men and women that often require him to spend and be spent. Tirelessness doesn't mean that he doesn't get tired, but that he is not dissatisfied to serve and give himself in service for the Lord's glory. His services will lead to moments of sorrow as well as moments of ecstasy. He will rejoice with some in their happiness and sympathize in tears with those whose hearts are saddened by the crisis of everyday living. It is impossible for those being served to compensate the man of God who serves with a heart of faithfulness to Christ. The personal knowledge that Jesus, the Chief Shepherd, will provide for his every need will sustain and encourage him at those moments when it seems physical and financial sustenance is far in the distance. The Lord has promised, "Therefore my beloved brethren be ye steadfast, unmovable always abounding in the work of the Lord for as much as ye know that your labour is not in vain in the Lord" (I Cor. 15:58).

The minister should never perform his work according to his salary. We readily apply the verse "the laborer is worthy of his hire," but with the minister, the work and not the money is of prime importance. Many in the gospel ministry must work in the secular world to provide adequately for their families, but this should be avoided if at all possible, especially if it hinders the minister's availability to his congregation and their needs. He must, however, take special effort and care not to use his position to accomplish or accumulate financial gain. It is wise for him to stay away from using his name for commercial purposes, keeping in mind the uniqueness of his office and the seriousness of his calling. The minister must hold his professional service in such high esteem that he will not allow it to become dissipated in the maze of service channels that funnel out in all directions today.

In his book, *Better Leaders for Your Church,* Mr. Weldon ably sums up the covenant of service for Christ and His church, which should also be the covenant of the Christian minister who is striving to produce service of the highest superiority. He says, "Christian stewardship is faith in a loving God at work in our world, a realization that all that we are and have is a gift in trust from Him, and the consecration of ourselves, together with our possessions, as co-workers with him. This faith, when practiced, becomes the motivating sense of responsibility for the Christian's well-being of our God-given world" (33).[3]

The height of his ministry is seen in winning souls to Christ. Because he is called to preach the "unsearchable riches of Christ Jesus," it should never become anything less than this.

# CHAPTER TWO

## The Minister as a Man

<u>1. His Physical Life:</u> Proper care of the body is of utmost importance to every individual. The minister should not fail to realize that only as long as his physical body is functioning properly will he be able to preach, serve, and reach the goals of his office. There will be times when the minister must put in many hours without sleep or relaxation, but he should plan his schedule so that he can have a definite time for rest and recreation. It is very important that the Christian minister do all in his power to keep his body fit and in the best condition possible so that he can perform to the highest the type of service belonging to God and His people. Jesus Himself recognized the imperatives of physical retreat for refreshment and rest. For personal spiritual rejuvenation, there must be physical stamina. This is not a resource we have in reserve; it is an action that must be taken in pursuit of calm, quiet, and replenishing. When we are invigorated, we are at peak performance capacity for the Master's service. However, this is the physical side of service; because we know to rely on God spiritually is to acknowledge our weakness, our ability to do or accomplish His will without His powers is an impossibility. But, this is one area we can take some responsibility over, in general: eat

right, watch our health, and exercise to a level that will promote good health without worshiping the body itself.

"Come ye yourselves apart into a desert place and rest awhile, for there were many coming and going and they had no leisure so much as to eat" (Mark 6:31 KJV). There is a real temptation to forgo regularly scheduled meals by many in ministry. The bustle and hurry of service and pastoral caring, not to be equated with the occasional chosen fasting, is negligence of nourishment. Jesus recognizes the human qualities that His created beings possess, and food is a necessity, as well as sleep and serene reflection in an uncluttered, distracting environment. Temperance and moderation is still application to physical engagements, both in service and in self-care.

2. His Mental Life: It has been said that the holiest men have been the most studious. The mental life is a very vital phase of the Christian minister. Laxity on this part has been the reason many have come to disrespect the relevancy of the Christian minister's impact on scholarly matters or adroitness in non-religious matters. We have a responsibility to the communities we serve, as their shepherds, not to allow the spiritual thrust of our lives to overshadow our call to relevancy in common, everyday events.

Jesus was deeply interested in the mental life of people with whom He was in contact daily, challenging them to think through spiritual matters as they applied to the routines of weekday, seasonal occupations in the earthly pursuit of living in the physical.

He often encountered those in an oppressed, deranged condition, and He restored them to mental healthiness. Freeing them to the capacity of intelligent reasoning, thinking, remembering, and choosing, He then imparted to them the spiritual appropriateness of knowing their Lord. Choosing good books for the progress and application of our work is very important. These materials represent the conscious and moral positions of persons who have the ability to influence some action in others. We are encouraged to view all we read in the light of God's Word, which determines the value of the entire piece and veracity of the wisdom exhibited in its content.

Christian ministers should be cautious that their moral sensitivity is not dulled by indulging in intoxicants or any mood altering substances. His mind should be definitely and absolutely committed to the Lord. He should also live in awareness that he has the power to discredit his ministry if he allows his personal achievements and accomplishments to cloud his servant role with pride of status and recognition. Power and prestige are very real dangers in the life of public servants, of which the minister is the chief of servants. Such stumbling blocks can preoccupy the minister's thoughts such that his time and effective service becomes tainted by a dogged sense of self, to the neglect of those whom he is called to serve. Our affections are to have but one goal: to promote and not to demote Jesus Christ.

As God's ministers, we must keep ourselves under control. Not exercising discipline over ourselves, but allowing unbridled passions, anger, violence, argumentative self-justification, and revenge seeking to steal our energies and spiritual growth, is to close our ministry before it has opened in gentle bud, and it will never blossom under our hands. We must realize that opposition, frustration, and deliberate malevolence can be a satanic fiery dart in the work we are pursuing, however faithfully and earnestly, God blessed and prospering. Clergy must avoid an *Invictus* attitude, insisting: "I am the master of my fate... captain of my soul" (Henley).[4] But, a greater call for moderation in applying temperance and discipline is a mandatory objective in which our affections must be unwaveringly set. These are the biblical virtues that will enhance us as well as those around us, and they will secure us in the attacks that will unavoidably arise. The mental health of the minister is always on display. He needs a reasonable degree of insight into his own weaknesses, and he must learn to turn them to his best advantage.

Setting a definite time for study keeps the minister in training for his task. Planning time for the activity of mental growth not only enlarges his scope of thought, but also provides a more intense orderliness in his daily management of the Lord's ministry. He can invoke a sense of structure and reliability in others when his life reflects order and priority in the purpose of his servant role. People sense whether or not preparedness is a part of the minister's life or compulsion. Is he managing director in administrative matters of his personal life as well as in his pastoral leadership aims? It is written that we are to "study to show thyself approved unto God, a workman that needeth not to be ashamed, rightly dividing the word of truth" (2 Tim. 2:15). This is an unbreakable instruction. We must be approved by God. So, we study the Bible and all that pertains to our understanding of its content. We are to be workmen that will not be ashamed or make others ashamed of us in our work as we rightly divide the word of truth. It takes practice and commitment that has been in effect all along to produce the results we seek. Study enables the minister to master subjects that are important in the development of himself and others. Subjects that will be a tremendous asset to his vocation are the Bible as well as history, sociology, biology, anthropology, psychology, philosophy, ethnology, and theology.

3. <u>His Spiritual Life and Duty</u>: A minister must strive towards the highest spiritual level that is possible in application of living as a man of God. It must not take on the character of an option; it should be a must. All the attainments that benefit those served will fit the verse of Zechariah, chapter 4, verse 6: "It is not by might, nor by power, but by my spirit, saith the Lord of hosts" without exception. When our soul's singular desire is saturated to the zenith of pleasing God, we will never lose the blessing of missed opportunity in our ministry.

The congregation cannot acquire or maintain a high standard of spiritual life with a mediocre leader. Hosea chapter 4, verse 9 informs us: "And there shall be, like people, like priest: and I will punish them for their ways, and reward them their doings." One essential facet of this verse is that it is lucid that the minister strive to live a consistent prayer life. He must keep in continual communication with Christ. In doing this, he will find that he is not only being blessed himself, but he is also an immeasurable blessing to others. This is a duty, but a pleasurable one if the mandate to pray is understood as a loving concourse with the One who is most concerned with our success, which is God's role.

A prayerful life has proven to be the key to unlocking the doors of blessings that God promises to open to us. Giving us all the benefits of Himself, He as the reward, the rewarder, and the refresher of ourselves, others, and all that matters to us.

4. <u>Duties to Home and Family</u>: A large number of Christian ministers have become undone due to unnecessary negligence in this area of priority. The unhappiness that flows from the marriage and family life of God's servants is a bitterness that spills over into his area of service. Attentive pastors will not become lax over such a serious area of his ministry. The Apostle Paul has given some of the most useful and essential guidelines regarding the requirements of leadership of

God's flock. He writes to Timothy in 1 Timothy, chapter 3, verse 5: "If a man does not know how to manage his own household, how can he care for God's church." The Apostle also wisely instructs that "if any provide not for his own, especially those of his own house, he hath denied the faith and is worse than an infidel." It is in this area of living that most ministers and ministries are brought to stagnation and a sulfuric demise. The husband-minister is first a minister in his own home and that ministry then extends to those in the congregation or his venue of service. It would be thought strange that a man could only see or hear the calls of a stranger for help and not hear the screams for help from those right within his home. But that is often the situation. Our vision can become so farsighted that whatever near is left unattended, and the problem at hand usually keeps those farther away from drawing closer. We must work diligently so that we insure and assure our partners and children that while we are their shepherd too, never are we not their Dads.

This area of the man of God's life is so important, and to neglect it is as great a threat to his ministry as the threat of personal laxity in spiritual and study habits. An unsupportive wife is a threat with the capacity to capsize a man's effectiveness in ministry. So, to look diligently into the needs of the family is crucial. A wife who is complaining, nagging, and openly fights with a pastor as he tries to exhibit loyalty to his flock and dispense his office with faithfulness to the Lord and the church can disrupt a lifetime of positive gain. Her insecurities must be allayed. The only way to do this is to pay attention to her needs for care and affection. The tenderness of acknowledging her value as wife, mother, or companion generates respect and a sense of security in the relationship. The pastor is exposed to many people with many needs; he cannot meet them all, but his wife's concerns are to be taken seriously, not swept into a side pocket and forgotten.

Women are primarily people who sense situations through their intuitive, emotional traits. This is a valuable and viable part of who they are. These traits assist them in avoiding bad relationships and in the protective care of themselves and others. For example, motherhood brings about a deep, intrinsic maternal protective behavior in well-adjusted women. If it has not been established where she and they fit into the ministry and its life, this can also lead to feelings of threat from a relationship that requires much of her husband's time away from her and the family. Knowing where the fit is prevents her from becoming negative towards the people in it. She will see their foibles and shortcomings as you, the spiritual leader, guide them towards growth and her responsibility to assist in prayer, encouragement, and support. Not to include her as an ally in loving your congregation to God will force her towards other outlets for her concerns or gifts. She may become overly critical of the ministering body, of the congregation, or towards you, the husband-pastor. She may develop a sense of unworthiness and become overly materialistic and self-indulgent. Sometimes she can become too controlling, feeling that her usefulness is being forced from her. What you want to strive for is an atmosphere of joy in service that flows from relationships in the home and extends to the people in the church. It is cyclic. A wife who is fully supportive, loving, and trustful of her mate will be genuine as she stands with her husband in his work; this gives her husband the freedom to do with all his heart what God called him to do (MacArthur, 371).[5]

5. Personal Finances: The Christian minister must take care that money is not allowed to control his life. Money in itself is not wrong, but we must exercise good judgment in how we use it and how we allow it to use us. We know that credit is the new rage, and to get it now, pay for it later is a dominant factor in the way markets earn their profits. But, the high cost of buying on time is extremely dangerous. It is easy to acquire the means to more, but the plastic still must be answered with dollars that are not so easily obtained. Credit induces us to overspend and to purchase things we do not really need, or have a purposeful need of. We can buy things just to occupy space or to pronounce to others that we have enough money to waste. However, good stewardship, or good sense in money matters, requires us to consider what money can do. Again, the trusty wisdom of Apostle Paul puts it into good sense and a right perspective; in 1 Timothy, chapter 6, verse 10 we read, "The love of money is the root of all evil: which while some coveted after, they have erred from the faith, and pierced themselves through with many sorrows." Avariciousness should be absolutely excluded from the character of the Christian minister. Its clutches can destroy him morally and spiritually, which will be detrimental to his profession. His standards should be of the highest in both speech and behavior.

Negligence in debt management is a bad reflection on the preacher. He must take care that all obligations and bills are paid in a timely, accurate manner. Consistency is a testimony towards one's honesty and reliability; no apologies are needed for that. How ever, since we cannot control circumstances, there may be a time when irregularity may disrupt our cash flow, impacting our ability to pay our obligations in a timely, consistent, and accurate manner. Then we must take all necessary steps to assure our creditors that we are willing to work within an arrangement suitable to them and us to eradicate any indebtedness we have to them. To exalt Christ is to be at the forefront of all we do, and so much so in our worldly obligations. Predominantly, the minister must avoid getting entangled in anything that will dampen his ability to win souls to Christ.

The minister may be encouraged to patronize a business through their offering of discounts. This is in order, but should be accepted when the discount is voluntarily. The man of God is never to solicit favor in the marketplace because of his vocation. Areas of service where the minister can accept fees are in the ceremonies that celebrate births, dedications, marriages, and memorials. He should avoid requiring charges for funerals. Gratuities are in order when offered and should be accepted to avoid offense. He should be sensitive of his role as clergy that it is his duty to render professional service whenever called upon, while keeping mind that his aim is to reflect Jesus in every effort.

# CHAPTER THREE

## The Minister as a Citizen

1. Civic Services: In civic services the minister is a great force in the local community, and a leader in civic affairs wherever he resides. He should also, like every other citizen, enjoy all the rights and privileges relating to citizenship. Since the minister is looked upon as an ambassador of God, his words are more highly valued than those of the ordinary local citizen. He is placed on an equal level with other public leaders, such as the judge, the doctor, lawyers, and other servants of public concerns.

The Christian minister is often required to render his services with public addresses or public prayers in civic and national assemblies. He should be aware of the fact that in these functions, his course of conduct and actions are somewhat different from his usual pulpit and parish procedures. He should be mindful not to use this opportunity as a means to promote his particular denomination, but he should understand that he is representing the entire Christian ministry. To wisely execute his calling and serve to the best of his ability, not partiality and preference is the suitable thing. It is to be considered an honor to be the select spokesman for the Church Universal, keeping in mind the uniqueness of this vocation.

However, in discharging the functions of public servant rather than a pastoral administration over his flock, it is always wise to consider whether the Biblical principles established by the Lord Jesus will be compromised if he agrees to serve in a public function. Generally, this is all the consideration that is necessary because the primary opportunity to point men to Jesus does not limit us to our houses of worship or door-to-door visitations.

2. Invocations at Public Meetings: Most public assemblies requesting clergy participation hope that he may dignify the gathering with a sense of seriousness and solemnity. To many, this is a most vital contribution, and it is held in very high esteem. This is not just a symbolic gesture, and it should not be considered as a waste of time. The man of God's involvement is to impress upon the people thoughts of god-consciousness. His close walk with God is key to any spiritual influence made upon those listening. With this link, it makes the Christian minister an important part of whatever transpires. The true Christian minister will realize this, knowing that he cannot deny himself or his God.

Many times the minister is put in an odd position in serving interfaith meetings and other gatherings of diverse religious creeds, causing a conflict with the definite affirmations his calling represents. When this does occur, we can stand with the Apostle Peter in his declaration that: "We ought to obey God rather than men" (Acts 5:29). Let this settle matters or prayerfully consider what good can be obtained from compromise.

In his book on *Ministerial Ethics,* Nolan B. Hannon asserts:

> The professional rule that under no circumstances may a minister forswear this ministerial calling or Christian character must be carefully observed on all public occasions. In the attempt to be a good fellow at the civic club luncheon there have been ministers whose stories and speeches were out of keeping with their profession. Such men lose far more than they gain and are marked down more than they realize by the very men they are trying to impress (Harmon 59).[6]

3. Privilege of Citizenship: As citizens, we who serve in ministry must also submit to the laws of the land as long as these laws do not conflict with our obligations to God.

As servants of God and citizens under governmental authority, we have the privilege to exercise our right to vote, complying with the proper rules and regulations enabling us to become a voter. It is wise to keep in mind that because politics have a type of inherent corruptness, that does not eliminate our duty to maintain good citizenship.

In addition to privileges that we enjoy as citizens, the ballot and the inalienable right to life, property, and the protection of the law, the minister also enjoys certain specific reserves afforded by the state. Because of the nature and understanding of the responsibilities of ministry or pastoral life in these United States, the minister is usually exempted from jury duty; this is an outgrowth of old English Common Law as it ascribed to the character of clerics as men of mercy and not of judgment. He is exempted from mandatory service in armed forces in times of war although he is not excluded from giving service in military branches. He is not summoned to serve; neither does the state force the minister to any other service which violates his conscience. Certainly, there is recognition given the minister by the state which is not given to the ordinary citizen. Mr. Harmon addresses this in his treatise also, stating:

> These privileges he should recognize as belonging to the sacred nature of his office, and he should accept them accordingly. In turn the ministry should pay back to his state his loyalty and his service in his distinctive way (Harmon 63).[7]

4. Political and Social Questions: Much care should be taken by clergy to avoid being drawn into situations that are highly political, but on which the minister may be considered an authority. His considerations should be centered on those questions on which the moral consequences may affect the lives of his people, whether he is in or out of the pulpit. Howbeit, moral questions sometimes have dual implications, and he must avoid being drawn into such issues. Neither should he base his decisions on hearsay. If the minister proposes to attack any issue, he should always substantiate his argument

with the facts. The author of *Ministerial Ethics,* Nolan B. Hannon approaches the possibility in this manner:

> The church should be a big factor in the life of today. Of what use is it, they say, to ignore the present pressing matters of bread and meat, right and wrong, human shame and degradation (Harmon 64).[8]

# CHAPTER FOUR

## The Pastoral Ministry

1. <u>Member Visitation:</u> This has been, and still is, a very important phase of the Christian ministry. This is not an easy task, taking time to call upon persons of diverse occupations, sexes, states of health, and manner of lifestyle, but it is an area requiring diligence on the part of the minister. Lack of personal interest and concern for members' well-being apart from their church attendance has been cause for some to lose trust in ministers and respect for the Church. Attention to the individual has proven to be a vital asset to the cause of Christ. It is a wise minister who purposely encourages personal discipleship and service in his members. The pastoral visitation strengthens the spirit of fellowship and unified purpose among the Body of Christ, and it will quell the temptation to compete for the pastor's favor.

On the other hand, the threat of inactivity and slackness regarding follow-up will cloud the greater objective of the growing disciple; their enthusiasm will be soon replaced with complacency and dullness. Churches do not thrive or attract others to its fellowship and life if disinterest and apathy is more apparent than the activity of the Holy Spirit. We ought to guard against this at all times. If we refuse to extend our ministry to personal pastoral care, we lose our Christian credibility.

If we were to contrast the office of the pastoral ministry, the office of apostles, prophets, and the evangelists may outrank the pastor ecclesiastically. However, the triumph remains in the hands of the man who goes in and out among his people visiting the sick, and binding the spiritually bruised and broken-hearted. A pastor's strength is renewed after seeing the growing believer in his common or natural domain, enjoying God at work in the routine places. It is an essential and very precious ministry.

In performing his pastoral duties, it is most important that the minister avoid showing any partiality. He cannot but endanger his effectiveness as pastor if he is selective towards whom he is to visit based upon likeable traits, economic status, and prestige. His ministry must be that of a servant whose heart is down-to-earth even while his head entertains loftier ideals. If it becomes necessary for him to wipe a sweaty brow, wash grimy feet, or put a napkin to a drooling mouth, he must not allow himself to behave as if he is above it. A good pastor, like a good parent or teacher, definitely has no right to act out of favoritism, even though he may have his favorites.

Jesus often spent time with his friends Lazarus, Mary, and Martha. He was known to be the friend of Lazarus and his sisters. Their home was known as the place where He spent a great deal of time. Obviously, He felt comfortable with the companionship of this family. The reasons are not offered for our understanding, but we simply know that these were persons with whom Jesus enjoyed spending pleasurable time. The Scripture assures that these were special friends: "Now Jesus loved Martha, and her sister, and Lazarus" (John 11:5). This very touching statement would imply that Jesus had favorites, and these friends were closer than His inner circle of ministers, called the twelve. However, throughout the Scriptural record, especially in the gospels, we see Him deliberately seeking, touching, sending, loving, serving, and spending time with others desiring his help. The servant is to be balanced and equal in socializing, in service, in ministry, in intercession, and in following up with his flock, whether they are ill or well. By doing this, the minister is modeling love in his professional discipline. He is Jesus to the generations filling the church. So, the minister's walk must be as much like Jesus' as possible.

Of course, there are those who will need special attention, such as the aged, the sick, the dying, and the distraught. Otherwise, he is to hold and serve his people equally.

In ministering to the same persons week-to-week, and year-to-year, it is quite natural that some families, persons, or person may gain a special place in the life of the pastor. Often, a wise and kindly deacon, church mother, and the persons who have a deep love for the fellowship and have spent many years serving can so easily translate their passion for the things of God into the spirit of the man of God, and it is most difficult not to have a deeper affection for such devout saints. Generally, these types of associations are very readily accepted because these are the pillars of the church who have been active in drawing and winning souls to the Lord and these know how to love the body of believers for who they will become, not for where they currently are. It is good for a pastor to develop a connection with saints who are well respected and revered for traits he would like to see emulated in the church at large, because these will be the persons to whom he can direct others for counsel and discipline when it is a matter not requiring pastoral intervention. With such relationships, it is good that the congregation know the pastor's views of any who are held in such affection; an occasion to divert members or persons to them will require a measure of confidence in their ability to meet the counselee's need.

2. <u>Office Calls:</u> The pastor should establish an atmosphere of availability and ready approachability within the congregation. His parishioners should have no reticence about coming to him for appropriate counsel. It is essential that the flock know that they are near and dear to the pastor. There are often some, because of shyness, the nature of their problems, extra sensitivity, who will hesitate coming openly to the church officer these are often people needing help the most. In such cases, the minister might consider seeing the person in a place and a time that assures them the utmost confidentiality and privacy. Yet, in doing this, the pastor must insure that he is not dispensing partiality, but extending a compassionate concern for the deep emotional and psychological sensitivity of the parishioner. The pastor may arrange for another trustworthy individual to

accompany him to a certain point and wait if the counselee is unwilling to have someone listen with the pastor; it is very important that the pastor assure confidentiality will be maintained, but it is his ethical duty to have another person in the session. Explained in this way, it is doubtful that the sincere person would refuse this arrangement. Personal accountability, when adamantly established, will be the building blocks for solid, reputable pastoral counseling. The world provides more persons with neurosis and emotional stresses than we can keep abreast of; reading and researching the psychological journals along with Bible study aides the minister in his work. Yet, nothing can replace diligent prayer and Biblical counsel.

Ministers must apply the rules of safety and common sense in attending every situation that calls for the pastor's intervention. There are domestic situations that may need a mediator to disarm a potentially violent or actively violent encounter between parishioners. Many spouses are having problems that have not been dealt with in an amicable manner, and they are dangerously violent and abusive. The church is not exempt from this malady. The stress levels of men and women are often at a breaking or boiling point, and there is very often an exchange of behavior not associated with Christian people.

Knowing when, where, and how to counsel persons with marital difficulty that is entangled in violence requires that the minister knows how to speak to the issue without infuriating the counselee or taking sides with one over the other. His point of reference must always be as God's spokesman who offers wiser counsel that will bring about positive, lasting results. Understanding that people in marital conflict will seldom be willing to give up their point of view or feelings of entitlement towards getting revenge over the offending party, except when there is a change of spirit and mind. The pastor must also recognize that a dangerously fragile situation may necessitate the removal of the most violent party, sometimes involving police, or providing safety and shelter for the most vulnerable.

With small children and often teens, there needs to be a way to provide safety and shelter for these tender lives. A shepherd who foresees the probability that anything that can attack the flock will, and he must, have networks of willing members and agencies in place to offer aid in such matters.

Often, pastors, who have served at other churches and whose new area of ministry is a direct result of some unfavorable circumstances in previous service, may be unaware of hostilities that cloud his demeanor, therefore producing an air of aloofness among the members. This can be a genuine threat to his receptivity as pastor and mentor. It is with this in mind that I encourage ministers to know themselves, know their own hearts by constantly examining their motives for ministry. Hurting people does not help other hurting people very well unless their hurts have been properly dealt with. Bitterness and disappointment do not always drive men from pulpits, but bitter men in pulpits will most certainly drive people away from them and the church.

The pastor's depth of understanding human personalities must be very well above average. He will do well to prayerfully consider emotional states and the reality of altered psychological make ups due to life's strains and the use of potent and harmful drugs, prescriptive and illegal. The area of ministry is certainly bringing forth many whose lives have been mutilated in some self inflicted form or due to duress that far outstrips maladies known in ministry over 30–35 years ago. The horizon is brimming with individuals escaping something deeper than the issues our seminaries dealt with during that period, but now seminaries are currently trying to find mechanisms that will bring these persons face to face with the gospel.

The active pastor, one who sees his pastorate as an extension of the area of missions and evangelism, can not escape dilemmas that plague the community he serves. Many times the schools that serve the neighborhoods are an exact sampling of the type of problems that reside in the community. The minister may get his first hand at counseling experience among the youth population. Even early signs of trouble in the church and community can surface among the young first. A problem with promiscuity generally appears at the school yard and then the church; however, it can be very much visa versa.

Youth and their drinking of alcohol, taking of drugs, and participation in bloody violence has placed many confused, hostile, and lonely young people into the church's hands. If done well, this can be the best thing happening to youth. Here they may receive a genuine explanation of who God is, what the gospel is about, and most importantly, how their lives can have the proper significance God says it should.

The church is still a rescue mission and ministry to those whom it is trying to save and return to society as whole individuals who will repeat the cycle in new lives. Youth need a new beginning that puts them in a better position to choose wisely. What they have presently is their understanding of life as they have been taught through the ruthless and reckless methods of film, television, and uncaring adults. The pastoral ministry is the provision for the correct, eternally benefiting, and satisfying change many youth are looking for. We must never overlook or sidestep this challenging area of ministry.

The Apostle Paul suggested sound advice to Timothy concerning the importance of knowing how to dispense counsel. In the age-relationship of a pastor to his elder parishioners, Paul says, "Rebuke not an elder, but entreat him as a father; and the younger men as brethren; the elder women as mothers, the younger women as sisters, with all purity" (1 Tim. 5:1-2). Adhering to this invaluable wisdom will eliminate many unforeseeable problems.

This advice is more valuable in ministry now when we consider the latest priest-parishioner scandals that are rocking sectors of Christianity. The misdeeds of anyone bearing titles associated with religion, especially Christianity, is held up as suspect for all. We must not allow our God-entrusted duty to uphold the principles of His character and of our Christ to lower our standard and our guard because evil chases us and temptation can entrap us all. Every shepherd must serve knowing that the people to whom he gives service are primarily being watched over by God, and the minister, as God's steward, will a answer stringently for any misdeeds done towards them.

The general understanding is that Jesus taught about offenses as offenses coming to those who follow Him, not from those who follow Him. In those Scriptures referring to recompense to those who "offend these little ones who believe in me" (Matthew 18:6-8), it is more in the proper understanding that those offending His little ones were already among them. Religious leaders are not exempt from this warning. Temptations in the flesh and personal interest are enemies of the clergy, and they must be brought under scrutiny of the Holy Spirit. Any pastor or minister unwilling to handle himself in the light of Christ's admonition not to offend the believing child of God's—of course, this does not mean children in the sense of adolescents, but as dependent, immature believers—should not be surprised when his own secret sins and habits manifest themselves to his undoing. Many ministers have disgraced this calling by refusing to allow the Holy Spirit to "root out" the known lusts, angers, and temptations.

Presently, we are embattled with the accusation that the church and its stand against homosexuality is preventing many honest, loving, and good-hearted people from enjoying the freedom expressed to believers in Christ. The argument has taken a wider sweep as those advocating homosexual rights inject that Christianity is biased and prejudiced. Their dissenters insist that the church promotes intolerance when its very reason for seeking refuge in America is that it has freedom in its religious expression. There are many who purport to be religious, Christian, that are facilitating this rebelliously aggressive fight against the church. In this group, we find the confused innocent who has been indoctrinated in schoolroom scenarios of anti-biblical propaganda to believe that equal rights as decreed in our Constitution demand that homosexuals are to be accepted in any area of the church and its ministry without stipulations or restrictions. This ministry is powerfully challenging because the Scriptures require that this issue gets handled in a manner that confronts the practitioner of homosexual behavior with the clear understanding that his or her behavior is against God and against the very nature of man. The minister has a duty to establish the principles of the Word and the dignity of the church's stand on the subject.

However, since we must indiscriminately minister the gospel's call to repent to every person, we are to seek avenues to reach, teach, counsel in truthfulness and shepherd compassionately persons living in this condition. There are living examples of persons set free from the bondage of homosexual sins, so we do not need to feel inadequate to this challenge. The application of known Scripture texts that clarify and convict, along with verses that invite and heal, will always fit the occasion to witness or counsel persons in this lifestyle. So, none need feel that this area requires expertise beyond them. If he obtains specific literature that is Biblically correct and faithful in witness this will truly enable the minister to provide assistance while trying to disengage souls in this bondage.

In counseling homosexuals, lesbians, and persons classified as bisexuals and transvestites, it does help to know as much as possible about the family relationship. It is possible that the person is in this alternative lifestyle because of disappointments and rebellion. Those in the midst of family disputes and rage will respond differently to counsel and offers of redemptive deliverance than others who feel that they were born that way or that they are experiencing their quest for what they feel is true love.

Even with these pernicious activities and the lawsuits that have assailed the church, we still must perform our duties as men with commitments to Him who is the True Living God. We must avail ourselves, our time, and our offices to the people we are called to serve. We must be doubly sure that our actions are above reproach. We are expected to be imitators of Jesus as well as His representatives.

The area of counseling which many find intimidating and often personally distasteful is in the area of sexually transmitted diseases. Many HIV and AIDS patients are still not visited with the amount of constancy as a person with a non-sexually related disease. This dilemma has placed a very high-risk block in the minds and hearts of even the most conscientious clergy. However, to their credit, many are standing with the patients and their families to the dire end. It is very wise to take precaution, but take Christ to these whose lives are on the edge of desperation. Many are still in the grips of sin and blame God for allowing them to get into this terminal condition, even while admitting that their actions placed them in the predicament. But, ministry is the most crucial thing at this point in a strained and tenuous existence. It is still very certain, apart from intervention from God, that these afflicted will depart life sooner than they contemplated. It is not brutal or unkind to pray and witness to these with an urgency conveying that the luxury of procrastination is over. "Desperately sick people do want to talk, when they have energy to do so," stresses Drs. Eugene Kennedy and Sara Charles in their part-nered-written work, *On Becoming a Counselor* (400).[9] They stress the merits of nonprofessional counsel when accompanied with a listening, caring attitude.

3. Relationship with Women: The active minister will find that it is unavoidable that he will be called upon to visit women quite often. It is almost impossible to exempt oneself from this area of ministry. Since it is an obvious observation, most, if not all, Christian congregations are comprised of more female members than males. However, the spiritual maturity of the pastor and his dedication and commitment to serve his church should assist him in equipping himself against the errors easily made by many in public service. Yet, taking heed to the wisdom passed down by others by word and example should bear some leverage when ministering to or counseling the women in our ministry.

It is not wise for any minister to overly utilize his time and attention with women in his care. Men and young people can sense that an inappropriate amount of interest is being given in that area, and it will be a great hindrance in trying to reach unsaved men and boys. The inappropriateness of a man's behavior, as well as a woman's behavior, is very easily detected by males and especially youth. Young girls often develop a special attachment to the pastor, since he represents the God they can only imagine, but not see. It is best that the ministry led by the men of God exemplifies the type of behavior complementary to his office: godly. Young males often see themselves being a man like the pastor, taking leadership, showing concern, and dominating situations that need a cool head and quick action. It is important that they feel the care and manly traits that will help them develop into well-adjusted men. If the behavior of the minister is not properly conducted towards the female members, it will create a cynical and spiteful attitude toward ministers, the church, and the things of God in general.

Of course, the minister should be seen as being just a human being, but he should be respected for the position he holds because he exemplifies the character of a person deserving to hold that office, and not in the office because the office exists. The attraction to ministry for those who are not saved is the multiple opportunities to exploit persons and satisfy perverse habits. The man who is called of God has the most stringent charge to guard against such evils.

People should be made aware that the congregation's make up places a special need in the minister's life. His elders, leaders, deacons, or spiritual teachers should be involved in the counseling process with the pastor. The married minister should insist that his wife accompany him on visits with female parishioners in the office or outside of the office. The pastoral capacity must reach young, old, sick, well, rich, poor, the great, and the small. Every effort that keeps Christ at center should be employed.

Keep the Biblical objective to exalt Jesus and present Him as the answer because He is, and assure the hearer that the best answer to their problem, long term and short term, can only be realized and truly beneficial when Jesus is placed in His deserved position as Lord of their lives. As ministers, we can easily become so personally engulfed with the magnitude of the problems that we can forget that the answer and the provision for these persons is not within our ability to bring to pass. It is God and God alone who can and will. We cannot allow our empathy to ingratiate the burden and scope of the problems to obliterate our role. We are vessels and channels of the Father Word. God is the facilitator of His own will, and the people we counsel must be encouraged to seek the Father's will.

The unmarried minister will find it well to be accompanied by someone, perhaps an older, spiritually mature female with a good reputation, another leader, or the teachers in the congregation who deal with women's issues. We must take Apostle Paul's sound advice, putting it into practice at every juncture, "not letting our good be evil spoken of" (Rom. 14:16). This warning is more than appropriate, considering the loose, immoral behavior of church members and clergy in these times.

4. Visiting the Sick: This area of pastoral duty is one which yields a rich harvest to the pastor. If conscientiously engaged in, he is always most welcome into the sick rooms of members and most nonmembers of his church. James D. Murch, author and former Methodist Pastor, had these timely insights to offer:

> One of the most important demands upon the time of the pastor is the visitation to the sick. It is both a duty and an opportunity—a duty of the good shepherd who guards his flock; an opportunity for proclaiming the glad tidings of the gospel.
>
> Visits should be brief, forenoon is the best time to call. Kindness, gentleness, cheerfulness, quietness, and sympathy should characterize the minister's approach.

The primary purpose of the call must be religious. Persons who are very feeble should not be obliged to carry on a conversation.

The minister should practice no deception on the sick concerning either their spiritual or physical welfare.

Prayer—brief, sympathetic in spirit, and gentle in tone—should almost always be offered. The reading of Scripture will depend largely upon the patient's condition.

Intrusion upon the physician's province is unethical.

Cleanliness in body and clothing will obviate unnecessary annoyance and discomfort to the patient.

Where poverty and want, squalor and degradation, are discovered, the minister should see to it that the needs of the sufferers are supplied in the name of Christ and the church (27-28).[10]

5. Comforting the Bereaved: When a person has just died, whether sick or not, and friends and kindred are gathered in sorrow around the lifeless body, the minister may appropriately call to offer his sympathy, read the words of comfort from the Bible, and offer prayer. It is usually the wishes of family if the deceased is a member of the church, to notify the pastor immediately that he may be present at the time the body is turned over to the mortician. However, there are always variations. If the pastor is there at the time of pronouncement of death, the initial trauma and pain may have been discussed, prayed about, and meditatively reconciled.

However, the comfort of having the pastor present can not be articulated for many at such times. And for a few, they would rather not have the minister present until the final ceremony. It should be gently approached and courteously handled in either situation. Nevertheless, the minister's part can not be overly stated. His work and words make a major difference in how the family grieves and releases their loved one.

After the funeral, the pastor's comfort is needed more than before. He should make his visits longer and longer until time and assurance allays the disquiet of loneliness; and grief's pain is submitted to the healing power of the Holy Spirit.

It is essential that a pastor know how to counsel those grieving. There are many helpful written works that are very good aids on reflection on the life and significance of the deceased. It can also reinforce the Bible's promises, especially if the individual was a believer, and reassure the family members that their grieving is as natural as any of the other processes we encounter in life.

Removing the stigma and often the questions of why it takes some longer to resolve the issue of grief and allowing the emotions of missing a loved one can be the quickest route to healing from the pain of loss. It is discouraging to insinuate or verbalize that sufficient time has elapsed and that the grieving should conclude. Timetables set by others for the persons experiencing loss can be more devastating than not allowing them to grieve because they are under criticism and need permission to empty the pain in a manner that is cathartic and therapeutic.

This is one area of pastoral ministry that calls for a man of expansive spiritual compassion and biblical knowledge. Healing comes through and from the Word, and it will do its job best when the minister actively and lovingly acts as facilitator in this healing.

6. Visiting the Jails or Prisons: Many ministers have been very lax in this very biblically substantiated area of pastoral ministry. When prison visitations are to be made by the minister, he should be extremely particular in compliance with the rules and regulations regarding prison visitation. He is to avoid any form of misunderstanding regarding the state's rights and his civil and clergy rights. It is of utmost importance that the nature of his work and the place of his function do not collide due to an assumption that his ministry to the community at large will be received in the same manner in a prison community. He may find resistance from the security personnel, as well as resistance from the inmate or inmates. To some in jail, religious figures are a reminder of cold, stern, and harsh dictatorial parents, especially fathers. To many in policing of prisons, clergy is seen as a foe to the service they perform to society, where the police are villains and the inmates are somehow hapless victims. Therefore, it is very important to establish a working respect with the official staff and a trust that will dispel hardness and resentment from the persons to whom you are trying to minister.

In the complete sense of ministry in this type of arrangement, the prison personnel are as much in need as those who are incarcerated. It is often reported that officers and guards have deep problems and unresolved distresses that surface as hostility and unusual force being applied. This is in no way to imply that most prisoners demand a harsh and grave response, and that anyone appearing weak may find themselves in trouble trying to serve the prison population. But, the man of God should have concern for the eternal condition of the guards as much as he does for the prisoners. This should not fail to be communicated and followed up with proper written statements and invitations to attend the worship, Bible studies, concerts, and special events. It would not be inappropriate to offer personal counsel and visitations.

It is the minister's desire to be looked upon as a compassionate, understanding, wise friend and counselor to the prisoner, even though the inmate has been convicted and incarcerated for a crime. The man of God is there to help both the police and the convicted, but his attitude should not be one of compromise, but as an able spiritual intercessor.

7. Charity and Appeal for Aid: A social service committee of the church should be given the responsibility of answering the physical needs of the community's less fortunate. This type of ministering requires persons of great tact and skill. It is to the pastor's credit to choose qualified persons to facilitate this valuable area of church work.

The pastor will be targeted by some "streetwise" and "cunning" folk making appeals with fraudulent impositions; he must be judicious enough to determine which are true and which are fictitious. The unaware clergy will find the resources and supplies being depleted while there are still many honest needs to be met. Most suppliants are not frauds, but to assume that there are none is to cripple the intents and purposes this aid is to serve. He will have to implement a system of checks and balances, a system of follow-up that is in line with gaining the soul, if unsaved, and to infusing a bond of partnering to alleviate the condition, rather than entrench the needy person in a no-way-out circumstance. Teaching people to become God-reliant and employment capable is a good practice for any ministry.

Nevertheless, to feed the hungry, clothe the naked, and care for the helpless is a joyful part of our life in Christ, and it must be kept in the forefront of our service that we do this "as unto the Lord" (Matt. 25:40).

# CHAPTER FIVE

## The Minister and Public Worship

1. Conduct in the Pulpit: The minister should be exemplary in his pulpit manners. He must come to his pulpit conscious that he is the ambassador of God to God's people. It is in His name that the minister is standing there at all. It is imperative that earnest heed is given to himself in the way in which he shows respect or lack of reverence to the task he is entrusted. What he chooses to say, in speech and in actions, determines how the worshippers receive and process the significance of what they are about to do. James D. Murch has an insightful passage in his book, *Christian Minister's Manual* regarding this topic:

> The Scriptural rule for this office is that everything should be done "in decency and in order." It is well to precede the service with a moment of communion with God.
>
> Leading the congregation in worship is the first task. If there is a regular form of service accepted by the Congregation it is well to follow it, guarding however against the danger of mere formalism.

Hymns should be announced distinctly. Occasionally one or more stanzas may be read impressively that the worshipers may be governed by one of two rules—either select portions germane to the subject of the sermon, or else such passages as may promote acceptable worship (16-17).[11]

The prayers, offering, announcements, and sermon should all harmonize with and add to the sense of the presence of God. Church members, strangers, and even scoffers should sense that something sacred and unusual is taking place, that this gathering is not about the routines of everyday commonality, but that the holiness and wonder of God is apparent in what is being done. This atmosphere is different from any that is found at any other place in the world.

2. Preparation: The minister's preparation has more to do with the attitude and atmosphere of worship than with preaching only. He must have a personal feeling of preparedness, which involves many things such as the reading of the Scripture lesson and leading the prayers.

3. Order of Service: The entire service, from the opening hymn to the benediction, should be built as one unit around a central theme. There can be no adequate religious expression apart from worship. Worship must create the atmosphere for Christian living. It establishes and maintains spiritual contact with God. It creates a right attitude and an equilibrium of mind. Worship service should be so arranged as to satisfy the greatest need of the soul; revealing the soul's experience to others. It should be able to increase one's faith and intensify the love and respect for things sacred, thus creating and enlarging Christian fellowship in the bonds of spiritual experience. This brings new courage, hope, and strength for the tasks and problems that are inherent in Christian living.

The minister should avoid ostentatious, elaborate orders of service. Emphasis should be placed on simplicity and the beauty of trusting in the True and Living God, and not on facility of ritual or ornate symbols. Unobtrusive, uncomplicated worship makes it possible for the participants to do all things "in decency and in order, according to God's will," and with "the spirit and with the understanding." It is important that the pastor or minister not lose sight of the principles of worship and are to be guided by reverence, dignity, order, simplicity, and adjustment to the needs of the people, honoring Christ, His Word and His church. Also, the allowance of the freedom of expression under the Holy Spirits impacts. Punctuality is to be observed to the highest degree. Facilitation of time frees the parishioners from unnecessary feelings of agitation and restlessness.

The minister should take an active part throughout the service because he is the leader of the praise. He encourages worshipers to take part with him in thanksgiving and celebration, which is actually why the congregation is mindful of the exhortation in the sermon. They have been led to the source, the reason, the wherefore of their being and purpose in life by a reverent, exuberant leader. Such a devout and orderly man of God will have little difficulty in leading a people exposed to such faith as this. They will gladly take his cue and embrace the Lord Jesus in worship.

4. The Sermon: The sermon should be prepared and delivered "in the fear of the Lord," observing the accepted rules of homiletics and public address. It should edify, inspire, and secure decisive action on the part of the hearers.

> Preaching is "spoken communication of divine truth with a view to persuasion, consisting of three vital elements, matter, manner, and the overall view to bring the hearer to a confident decision of agreement with God in obedient, active faith. The matter of the sermon should be Divine Truth. The manner—spoken, accompanied with illustration—where appropriate. And it's ultimate view, as before stated, is casting down the hostile, or doubtful mind against God, persuading them to embrace by faith, the Lord Jesus" (Pattison, 3).[12]

The sermon should be positive, in touch with God and man. It must have a direct influence on the conscience and be interesting in its content. The preacher will do well to be true to his own personality, not imitate another's style of oratory-delivery, which might expose him to be insecure and even as insincere. His complete presentation should be clear, well-thought out, and as fully detailed (researched) as possible. Every sermon should be made alive through prayer before bringing it to the congregation.

5. Conclusion of the Service: It is very much in order to conclude the sermon with a brief prayer, coinciding with the theme of the discourse. This is usually followed by an invitation to the unchurched to become a disciple of Our Lord Jesus. Messages preached to congregations that often have nonmembers must have a section that brings these face to face with the redemptive work of Jesus. The atonement work must be presented and explained with clarity of the purpose of such a necessary sacrifice and of man's required response as dictated by God. Often there is the notion that the objective of the service and the sermon has been met if the prayers were moving, the singing inspiring, and the message rousing and impeccably delivered. The real work of preaching is often telling when the congregation's reaction is visibly registered. The reaction in the congregation may be reflective; a prior soul in distress may reflect new hope and a spirit of joy. But, we are forever prayerfully hopeful that the unsaved find themselves in a relationship with the Lord. Then it may be said the objective of the sermon has been reached.

If there are any candidates for discipleship the church takes the position of its agreed upon method of bringing candidates into a relationship with the particular fellowshipping body. Some do this by voting, others by committee, board, or teaching classes, and then an induction of the disciple into the church. However it is done, the ultimate is to turn men from rebellion to righteousness, from sinner to saint, as per Jesus' commission.

The last phase of the service, the benediction, is generally given by the minister in charge, any other minister, or a designated individual. Some religious services require strict silence when its worshipers are recessing the sanctuary; others exit in a song of fellowship coupled with a warm handshake from the pastor and attending clergy. Either way, there should always be a sense of the "communion of saints," that the worship has indeed met its purpose.

# CHAPTER SIX

## The Minister and Public Functions

<u>1. Funerals:</u> The funeral offers a sacred opportunity for the minister to render a service of counsel and consolation. It is one of his most important pastoral duties.

The minister is seldom consulted as to the time, place, or conditions of funerals. Usually, the arrangements are all made before he is notified and requested to attend. This is a mistake. He ought to be conferred with in respect to the matter, before the arrangements are fixed.

Christian author James D. Murch makes a concise observation regarding instructions for funerals:

> It is never the minister's place to invite himself to this delicate service. The family or the funeral director should request his presence and notify him of the date and hour.
>
> A call at the home of the deceased should be made on the afternoon of the day preceding the funeral, to determine the desires of the family concerning music, obituary, etc. Sometimes, however, this information can be secured by others.

The funeral director should be consulted immediately preceding the services to determine any late changes in plans, the place to be occupied by the speaker, seating arrangement for the sinners (if the funeral is held from the home), and frequently the part to be taken by fraternal orders, etc.

The program of ceremonies should be brief (not to exceed thirty minutes) and in somewhat in the following order: (1) Song, (2) reading and prayer (3) song, (4) obituary, (5) sermon, and (6) song. Often all music is omitted by request of the family.

Obituaries should be prepared in advance and carefully read for proper pronunciation of names and places. The following information is important: (1) Date of birth, marriage, and passing, (2) age, (3) residence or occupation, (4) relation to Christ, (5) number of relatives remaining, (6) complimentary mention.

When all is in readiness the funeral director will signal the minister and the ceremonies are in his hands. The singers (previously acquainted with the program) will need only a signal from the minister to know they are to begin. At the close of the service the director will again take charge, until time for the committal.

The position of the minister in processions is important. If the funeral is held in the church he should call at the home at an agreed time and accompany the procession to the church. When the pallbearers bear the casket to the waiting car the minister should step out first and approach the car a few paces in advance of the casket. When within a few feet of the car, he should step aside, facing the casket as it is placed in the hearse. His car will be waiting near. He will enter it and take his place in the cortege. At the church he will greet it as it is removed from the hearse, turn and slowly lead the procession into the building, passing slowly to the pulpit. After the service, the minister does as before, in the procession, leaving the church and at the grave side. Approaching the head of the grave, he should pass on to the foot, where he will face about and give room for the pallbearers and the director to place the casket and make ready for the committal service. From this point, the minister will conduct the committal (facing the bereaved), and pronounce the benediction (107, 108).[13]

2. Marriages: Marriage is an order of creation and should therefore be regulated by the Word of God. It is the highest fulfillment of human friendship, filling every ideal of human intimacy, mutuality, and loyalty. It is one in which husband and wife covenant together with God that they shall in unity fulfill His purpose to the end of their days. For this reason, the Christian minister should confer with the couple and instruct them regarding the sacredness of this institution. The minister should never perform a ceremony where a believer marries an unbeliever. This will endanger the Christian's witness and make void the purpose for which it was instituted.

The gross sin of being unequally yoked has placed on the church an accusation from the world as false and hypocritical; we have not been as adamant about this most important ministry. Marriage is as much a ministry as proclaiming the Word is ministry. The church is in moral crisis because we, the pastors and ministers, have been inadequate in insisting upon adhering to the Scriptural methods of entering into the bonds of marriage. The result is that our churches are overwhelmingly and disproportionately filled with broken marriages and broken, hurting people.

The women of a marrying age are not as likely to consult the pastor regarding her life's mate in the non-Catholic churches. Fundamental and Protestant churches are less likely to require prenuptial counseling. Many engaged couples plan and prepare their wedding ceremony and notify the minister at a later date to request his participation in carrying out the ceremony only. This is a mistake of grave consequences. Pastors and ministers must take an active part at the onset of the engagement period. There are some churches that are now becoming more teaching oriented, and they have taken the reigns regarding its congregation and their life choices. It is with God's command to provide counsel in training children, and the children ought to be continually trained in making sound choices, especially in choosing professions and life-mates.

Armed with facts from experience and observation, each minister must be undaunted in approaching the subject of how our younger members develop a strong, healthy, and sound faith. When we delay building into them moral character and equipping the young with certainty and time-tested proofs that there are absolutes and that these proofs are supported by the most reliable source available, the Bible, then we will not have persons in the Body who are capable of training others in these same principles.

Ministers who are doing pre-nuptial counseling realize that it is often a time of enlightenment for the couple itself. Many couples are so enamored with the idea of being in love, they have never really gotten to know each other as individuals. There are simple, yet thought provoking materials that provide self-tests and studies on matters such as handling money, conflict, responsibilities, and personality issues. These are designed in such a way that the heart is exposed to the everyday issues that eliminate the manipulation of the emotional self.

The church must take active parts in the physical and the mundane, as well as the spiritual development of our developing parishioners. It is not enough to apply ointment to wounds; preventing these wounds is why we take the preventive measures of arming people with God's truth.

It would be easy to preach to those who are only doing well and doing the right things commanded in God's Word. But, we are who we are, sinners faced with the failures of our ungodly choices and trying to recoup our place in the family of faith. There are those who have experienced the trauma of broken family ties, have been born with no such ties, are single mothers or fathers, and are single because they did not choose to choose their life's mate according to the plan of God. Now, the minister must amply feed these needy sheep with the same life-giving Word, but often with a greater insight and awareness that the condition of the broken, fragmented, and non-existent family structure is not unique to this time.

There has been much controversy and discussion regarding the place of service and ministry to persons remaining or returning to the church with issues of divorce, single parenting, and remarriage issues, struggling to live out their faith and feel accepted in the Body of Christ. Whatever a minister feels compelled to do, he must fully acquaint himself with the Biblical perspective regarding issues of restoration, forgiveness, and places of services for persons impacted by these not so uncommon issues.

John MacArthur, Jr. speaks about outreach in his book, *Rediscovering Pastoral Ministry,* indicating that outreach does not take place only to those outside, but does also encompass those within the family of God (81).[14] Prayer to heal their hurts, forgiveness, reconciliation, and invitation to worship is to all. The matter of who should be in certain areas of ministry or leadership may need deeper insights into the Word of God and counseling. It is never shortsighted to bathe all concerns in fervent prayer, regardless of how one feels about the situation presented. However, it is always right to act in accordance to the written Word.

3. Baptism and Communion Services: Baptism is derived from the Greek word "baptizo," meaning to "dip," "plunge," or "immerse" for the purpose of dying. It can never mean sprinkling, or pouring.

To this symbolic significance of the objective manifestation of the believer's acquiescence to that relationship, here depicts the three steps: immersion—going into the water; submersion—going under the water; and commersion—coming out of the water. These parallel the concepts of entering into the death of Christ, experiencing the forgiveness of sins and rising, and walking in the newness of Christ's resurrected life. Baptism is done in the name of the Father, the Son, and the Holy Spirit (Matt. 28:19).

The Lord's Supper, called also the Eucharist and the Communion, is the most sacred act of Christian worship, and it is the highest expression of the mysteries of our holy religion. The Communion service should be led by the minister stressing that the supper is to "show forth the Lord's death until He comes," as set forth in 1 Corinthians chapter 11, verses 23-28.

The Communion service is a divinely appointed medium through which the Christian receives spiritual energy and is made radiant for service. Here the devout soul has contact with God, remembers the death and suffering of his Saviour, examines himself, asks for wholeness of body, soul, and spirit, and renews his covenant relationship. It should be observed without pageantry or ostentation, yet decently and in order.

4. Conferences and Conventions: The moral characteristics of the Christian minister should be of such that all his decisions are made

in light of the Word of God. Therefore, the opinion of the majority should not carry unless so decided.

This truth is emphatic and should be the prevailing line of demarcation, be it at a single conference or a major convention.

Some religious bodies are regulated and governed by conferences and conventions; others are self-governing with their power structures embedded within the body.

Conferences and conventions play an important part in presenting ideas that improve our individual church bodies. They are also instrumental in meeting new saints and fellowshipping with others. They are also a financial help to the smaller bodies that are less financially secure. Mostly, there is a coming together to magnify and glorify the name of our Lord, Master, and Saviour.

Many congregations, strongly attached to leadership of convention heads who draft decisions and regulations that get funneled down to the local church, are in dissent over issues in which they would prefer not to become involved. The convention can be a source of spiritual reinforcement, but if the direction being provided by its major leaders is causing a church to compromise its stand on biblical truth, then that convention and its leadership should not impact the infrastructure of a faithful, Christ honoring church.

At present, many Protestant churches are embroiled in arguments that are breaking it into factions. The issue of practicing homosexuals serving in pastorship and ministry has touched off argument and strained relationships within the body of believers. The long-standing argument of women in preaching and pastoral ministry still dogs many congregations, and it has caused much confusion because the leadership in the convention structure has agreed that these questions should be answered by their more enlightened views.

Conventions governed by biblical mandates in their teaching and opinions are valuable in the service it provides. They should never usurp the responsible leadership of the local body if that local body is acting in faithful ministry with the Bible as its superlative guide.

# CHAPTER SEVEN

## The Minister and Deportment

1. In the Home: The man of God must strive to maintain God's perspective on how he should deport himself in the home. The home is the acid test for the minister. If his children can look up to him and desire to be like him, it is a great honor because it indicates that he has lived a God-pleasing life. He should act as a shepherd to his children, not lording over them, but as an example before them. It is very important that the minister conduct himself as a Christian at all times. The better the father, the better the pastor, and the better the guide for the children, not only his own children, but other people's children as well. The minister should always remember that there are many pastorates and many church members, but there is only one home.

Ministry to the members in the home is not to be neglected. When the man of God begins his worshipful expressions with his wife and children in the home, it establishes the unshakeable foundation in the hearts of his family members that he is a man to take seriously, a servant worthy of obedience and honor. It will reflect in the pulpit and to the church at large that this man of God believes that God is truly his Lord. A minister on his knees in humble prayer stirs a spirit of worship and reverence in the heart of his parishioners; that is if he is truly a man of worship.

As a man of God pours himself into the family that God has given him, whether it is with his wife or with children alone, he can not do less than succeed. Where else would two like minds find that their energies are like "iron that sharpens iron" but together in committed prayer and worship of the God they both love.

Men of God must realize that the call does not mean that he becomes the spirit of God and must abide in the church building, but rather that he is a "man" of God, and the God who called him expects him to exercise his manly duties: to husband the wife and, if there are children, to father those children, as a man. The husband-man-of-God needs to remember that his help mate will welcome the opportunities to help when he makes the home a place of godliness too. It does not mean that he enters in with an air of righteous exclusivity, monk-like, but that the joy of the Lord should be evidenced at home also. He is to be a fruit of the spirit man of God when he is reclining in the living-room, retiring to the bedroom, and trekking back and forth among those most familiar to him and with his ways (MacArthur, 160–161).[14]

2. In the Church: Dr. Andrew Blackwood, author of *Pastoral Leadership,* offers this timely counsel:

> In an ideal setup, the government of the church rests with a single body. Usually it goes under the name of an official board; sometimes it is called a church council, or pastor's cabinet. This way of working calls for centralized authority, with as much diversity of function as local needs require. The stress falls on the team work of the everlasting whole. Under favorable conditions such a system gives the work of the church a sense of unity. The plan leads representatives of various societies and groups to become acquainted with each other and with the different activities of the church. All of this, to be sure, does not come of itself. It calls for skillful leadership on the part of the minister, and for loyal teamwork on the part of lay leaders (65–168).[15]

3. In the Pulpit : Nolan B. Harmon, in *Ministerial Ethics,* says, "A man's clothing and appearance always reflects his personality, and the minister is no exception"(198).[16] However, in some geographic locations and economies this statement will seem ill-fit as insightful commentary on appearance. However, in particular application to ministers in an economy as affluent as America, the notion is accepted that dress should be more defined and discrete.

Personal hygiene is never to be neglected, and cleanliness in our attire is an essential. Dress that is flashy, worldly, or detracting from the message places the focal on the person, and this is always out of order.

The robe is considered appropriate, formal attire on church occasions while unobtrusive clothing should be worn for general appearances. Usually, dark colored clothing is associated with sober-minded, serious, and grave temperaments with important functions. Also, transitions from formal settings can easily be made when the garments are not so unusual. However, many of the traditions of church worship are becoming so casual that jeans and sneakers are accepted as appropriate for worship in some settings. So, this matter is best placed in the context as to whom a particular ministry is being directed and to what degree is dress a matter of importance. We know that, ultimately, the worship is about converted hearts, disciplined lives, and faithful workers in the Kingdom of Christ.

*Pulpit Language:* The minister should be very judicious in his choice of language used in the pulpit. His speech should be governed by ministerial ethics, and he should always bear in mind that he is a representative of the Lord Jesus Christ. Whatever is said is to be for the purpose of maintaining the credibility of the profession of gospel preaching.

*Assertion and Remarks:* These should not be offered perniciously, but genuinely, for the edifying of the body of Christ.

*What to Say and Not to Say:* The minister should be the best guardian of his title at all times. It will help to remember the words of the Apostle James:

> But the tongue can no man tame; it is an unruly evil. Full of
> deadly poison. The wisdom that is from above is first pure,
> then peaceable, gentle, and easy to be entreated, full of mercy

and good fruits, without partiality and without hypocrisy. And the fruit of righteousness is sown in peace of them that make peace (James 3:8,17,18).

*Speech, Attitude, Toward Other Pulpits:* It is a breach of Christian ethics to speak unfavorably of a fellow minister for "we are laborers together" for Jesus Christ. "Christ is not divided, but...all speak the same thing, and that there be no divisions among you, but be perfectly joined together in the same mind and in the same judgment" (2 Cor. 1:10).

The Christian minister's attitude toward his brother minister is in a high degree indicative of his fitness for this Christly calling. There are certain inescapable obligations which he owes to his brethren. Usually, he has entered into other men's labors, and without much doubt, he will also have successors.

# Chapter Eight

## The Minister and Evangelism

1. Personal Evangelism:

> Andrew first findeth his own brother Simon and saith to him, we have found the Messiah...and he brought him to Jesus. Phillip findeth Nathaniel and saith unto him we have found Him of whom Moses in the law and the Prophets did write (John 1:41–45).

Personal evangelism has proven to be one of the most effective methods of soul-winning in the Christian church. This method can be utilized by the ministering pastor as well. Christ has left us no other plan; as we are won to Him we in turn win others to Him. Every believer has some important function to perform in the Master's vineyard, and He has given spiritual gifts and fitness according to his ability for that work.

Service is the object of personal divine life, and no soul is satisfied without it. It is the purpose of God in calling us. A Christian should possess the inward passion of his Master to see souls saved, for He was exceedingly concerned. Very often He prayed all night; He wept over Jerusalem; and His sweat was as drops of blood under the weight of His mission.

Success in the field of personal evangelism depends largely upon the evangelist's call by God, for it is a divine undertaking. Also important is his preparation for the task coupled with a mark of gravity and humility, a spirit-filled life and utter dependence upon Christ. For he clearly stated in John, chapter 15 in verse 5: "I am the vine ye are the branches; He that abideth in me and I in him the same bringeth forth much fruit: for without me ye can do nothing."

The awkward state of organizing and prioritizing those matters associated with directing and administering the things of God to the body of believers can so occupy a minister's time that personal evangelism is compromised and left off his schedule completely. However, many requests to attend affairs, to gather at ceremonies, and to speak at numerous events can seem like evangelist work when it really is diversionary tactics set in motion by the adversary. The people seeking to engage the minister most likely are folk known to him, and the real, underlying manipulator is never recognized. Therefore, it is dire that the man of God know what he is in ministry to achieve and pursue it with diligence. It is very easy to become diverted from those spiritual works that draw men and women to Jesus.

The minister is expected to engage men in conversation regarding God. Even unsaved persons expect the minister to put them on the spot. After all, the title he wears and the authority he exercises place him in the inarguable position to be the proper person to encroach upon another's private thoughts. In many third world and African American communities, it is expected that the "preacher" will talk about Jesus to the community. There is an advantage to having that given privilege. Our title puts us in the favorable light of being expected to talk about God. However, the shrewd spirit of secular humanism has detected this privilege, and it is determined to detach it from the minds of youngsters, men, and women. Schools are actively suppressing the earnest interest of students in the area of Christianity. The matters of spirituality are not being squashed, but the knowledge of biblical Christianity is being ridiculed, suppressed, and outright forbidden.

It is very important that the minister exercise his appointed calling to seek the lost, reach the lost with the Word of God. He has the authority and the equipment, and it is not wise to neglect or disregard this opportunity.

2. Evangelism in the Local Church: The Lord Jesus Christ, viewing the ripened harvest fields of His day among His own, said to His disciples "the harvest truly is great, but the labourers are few: pray ye therefore the Lord of the harvest that He would send forth labourers into the harvest" (Luke 10:2).

Andrew Blackwood, author of *Pastoral Leadership,* said, "The fields stand waiting for the harvest by an evangelistic church" (83).[17] Surely all churches should positively be evangelistic; its message and programs should be highly evangelical in outreach.

The pastor and people that are engaged in such a ministry prove to be the most progressive. The believer's spiritual life is kept renewed, and there is always the presence of the Holy Spirit moving in the church and community. Whenever sinners visit the church, they are challenged seriously to consider the value of their souls, which ultimately leads to the growth of the church. This, of course, is dependent upon the wise pastor who has proven to be evangelistic, so he must lead his people accordingly.

3. Evangelism in the Community: Care should be taken in this important phase of evangelism. Christ, in the sending forth of the twelve, gave them power and authority over all devils to cast them out and to cure diseases (Luke 9:1–2). So, also, these that do community evangelism must be so authorized and empowered that when the eventualities arise, they'll be able to master the situation. The disciples reported when they returned, that even the devils were subjected to them "through Thy name" (Luke 10:17). "Therefore, careful planning, much prayer and consecration, and waiting upon the Lord is of vital importance, since it is not might or by power but by my Spirit, saith the Lord" (Zach. 4:6).

The results of community evangelism are so meager at times because the efforts put forth are limited. The Holy Spirit is still bestowing gifts and as the Apostle Paul says, "covet or desire eagerly the best gift" (1 Cor.12:31), "for God giveth to all men liberally and upbraided not" (James 1:5).

Communities in many cities are comprised of many cultural groups that add interest and spiritual fervor to the church. We should never hesitate to share the gospel with another because they do not look like us. Perhaps a language difficulty on the part of the church could be remedied by taking classes in the prominent language, finding someone who can speak the language, or best yet, teaching members in the church. This is also a part of equipping the church. We must prepare to meet the challenges of culture and language in order that the gospel reaches its intended audience. God has given us the mandate through Jesus to take His gospel to every nation. Perhaps those of us living in areas where the cultures are diverse, God is reminding us that our hesitancy to go and preach to those who are not yet saved has been somewhat remedied. He has shortened the distance; they are now here.

There could never be too much said about community evangelism. The people living in closest proximity should be able to see Christ at work in the lives of believers. This is a prime area service. If communities are going to know Christ, it will be the light of those born of Christ shining clearly. This is a must. God deserves our reverence and obedience without unreasonable delay. The community needs to know the church that is of Christ is actively seeking to give it the best gift it could ever have. The benefits to a community that has the church on its side is a blessed community indeed.

4. World-Wide Evangelism and Mission: The last commission Christ gave to His disciple before He was taken up to heaven as is recorded in the book of Acts chapter 1, verse 8 is to be literally applied, "Ye shall be witnesses unto me both in Jerusalem, and in all Judea, and in Samaria and unto the utmost parts of the earth." The Apostolic church approved world-wide missions and evangelism; they started at home, then into the community and then worldwide (Acts 8:15-16; 13:1-4). It gave its best in leader's support and prayers, and it sealed the cause with its blood. The ministry of the early church was intensified by persecution. Its history proves that worldwide evangelism and missions are always advanced through persecution, or a period of systematic inflicting of punishment for adherence to a particular religious belief. This is chronicled as historical data in the *Zondervan Pictorial Bible Dictionary* by Merrill Tenney:

Persecution began as a social reaction by policy of repression was intermittent and became political later. The State's; and as the evidence of Tertullian shows number of Christians (637).[18]

The great Apostle to the Gentiles with his invaluable contribution to worldwide evangelism and missions—the Apostle Paul, being Saul of Tarsus at the time—appeared for the time in Acts chapter 7, verse 50 as a young man, already an acknowledged leader in Judaism. His active opposition to Christianity marked him as the natural leader of the persecution that arose upon the death of Stephen. The persecution described in Acts chapter 26, verses 10–11 indicates his fanatical devotion to Judaism. As Christians spread to other cities and their faithful testimonies increased the number of Jewish converts, this angered Saul and other Judaizers. As the persecutor of Christians, armed with authority from the high priest, approached Damascus, the transforming crisis of his life occurred. Saul at once saw the error of his way and surrendered instantaneously and completely. The new convert proclaimed the deity and Messiahship of Jesus in the Jewish synagogues of Damascus. His contribution to worldwide evangelism and missions included all the difficulties of path: suffering, privations, shipwreck, imprisonment, stocks, scourging, and unfaithfulness of brethren. His achievement proclaims him an excellent missionary statesman. His labors firmly planted churches in the strategic centers of Galatia, Asia, Macedonia, and Achaia while he planned to work at Rome and in Spain, revealing his imperial missionary strategy.

Our mission to win souls may not take us any further than the familiar geographic area of our towns and cities. But, the call to evangelize is still fresh and is to obeyed. Often pastors and ministers may wonder about the members who do not seek to win souls more often. There is a noticeable lack of involvement in witnessing and discipleship ministry among church members because the examples given from leadership is often not there. If there is to be a going out to win souls, the pulpit must provide the direction and guidance on how to go about getting there. Some would witness if they felt that they were doing it properly; there is no one entrusted with generating the enthusiasm and breaking open the truths of Scripture like the pastor.

Our outreach for worldwide evangelism and missions should be illumined with the spirit and determination of this great missionary, fulfilling the great commission of Jesus Christ: "Go ye into all the world and preach the gospel."

In bringing this discussion to a close, I conclude that the Christian ministry is esteemed as the noblest of all professions. The Christian minister must hold his calling in very high regard, striving to maintain all the virtues and behaviors that Jesus ordained that we must. We have no finer example than Paul, who continually persevered towards taking hold, apprehending the treasure of fullness in Christ. Every God ordained pastor must possess a strong mental and spiritual determination that will make him a true asset to society. One, by his example, proves to be a genuine defender of the faith by confirming the objectives and goals of his service in Christian leadership towards change in man's spiritual destiny. All efforts of missions and ministry should point directly to Christ and not to the servant—to the Shepherd, the One who appoints and shepherds whom He has chosen (Jeremiah 23:4).

# CHAPTER NINE

## Permissiveness in the Church

We are living in a time where the church seems to be losing her spiritual credibility. The Word of God is not honored as it should. The holy writ makes it clear that we are, as stated in the Sermon on the Mount recorded in Matthew's gospel chapter 5, verses 14–16, the salt of the earth and the light of the world. I strongly believe that the greatest problem in our churches today is the professors outnumbering the possessors. Instead of the world imitating the church, it looks as though it is the reverse; the church seems to be taking on the ways of the world. We need to take heed to John chapter 17, verse 16: we are not of this world; our citizenship is in Heaven although we are in the world.

In many of our congregations the name church has been dropped, substituted by the words center or assembly. Jesus made it clear in Matthew chapter 16, verse 18 that He established the "church." The church is not a center. In Matthew chapter 5, verse 18, our Lord made it clear that even if Heaven and Earth pass away, His Word will stand. Again, in Revelation, chapter 22, verses 18 and 19 there is a warning against adding or detracting from God's Word. In 1 Timothy chapter 2, verse 9, women are to "adorn themselves in modest apparel." They are to be dressed modestly, decorously, neatly, and pleasantly, not in such a way as to draw special attention to themselves and their appearance.

Many of our mainline denominations are permitting women leadership in our congregations. 1 Timothy chapter 2, verses 11–15 clearly stipulate this prohibition. Biblical headship is clearly stated in the scriptures. The three tremendous institutions God brought into existence are the home, human government, and the church, in that order. The divine paradigm is seen within the Trinity. Christ exercises headship over and in the universal church, local church, and the family. Each member of the Godhead is co-eternal, co-equal, and co-existent. They are of the same divine essence. God is one in three and three in one. The male gender is used in referring to the Godhead. In so doing, God is demonstrating that there should be masculine leadership both in the home and in the church. Nevertheless, between the office and role or function of each person, Jesus willingly submitted to that headship as stated in John chapter 14, verse 28, "My Father is greater than I." So, we see Jesus condescended to take on human flesh (Phil. 2:6-8) in order to become our substitute, so that He could pay for our sins. This doesn't make Christ in any way inferior in essence to God the Father. The Father sent the Son, who, of His own accord, submitted to take on the garb of humanity and humble Himself to the point of dying on the cross. One of the major passages supporting biblical headship is found in 1 Corinthians chapter 11, verse 3: "But I would have you know, that the head of every man is Christ; and the head of every woman is the man; and the head of Christ is God." This is a clear affirmation of headship with the Godhead.

The church, according to scripture, denotes Christ's Body (Colossians 1:18), which is often referred to as the universal church. And Scripture likewise speaks of the local church. Christ is the head of both. He definitely has that right because He founded the church (Matt. 16:18-20, Eph. 2:20). As the resurrected and exalted head of the church, Christ directs it. He directs the church through the Scriptures. God's Spirit employs the Word of God to convict, bringing the lost into God's church and providing guidance in their living, which results in service to Him. That's why it's ludicrous for human beings to take this credit. The church was purchased with Christ's precious blood, making Him the exalted head of the church. Those who have been redeemed only function as his vice-regents in the local church.

The Bible is crystal clear about headship in the local church. As elder, bishop, or pastor (1 Tim. 2:12, 1 Tim. 3:2), the word "bishop" or overseer" is in the masculine gender, which can only refer to a man. The Apostle Paul provided, under the inspiration of the Holy Spirit, two reasons why women are not to have doctrinal authority over men in the local church. First, he points out God's order in creation. God created Adam first; then from Adam's side, he created Eve. So, God created the woman for the man, not the man for the woman (1 Cor. 11:9). Genesis chapter 5, verse 2 views man as the general head of the human race. Secondly, Eve, not Adam, was deceived by the Serpent. This does not mean superiority, nor inferiority, but priority. This has to do with God's chain of command. According to Romans chapter 5, verse 19, Eve took the role of headship instead of subordination when she ate the forbidden fruit.

Scripture also teaches that the husband's headship is in the home. She is commanded from Scripture to submit to his authority, as stated in Ephesians chapter 5, verses 21-25. Also, Colossians chapter 3, verses 18-19 summarizes this great biblical truth. It cannot be stressed too strongly that the biblical teaching on the role of women in the church and home in no way implies the inferiority of the woman. From God's perspective, male and female are of equal value. He simply gave them different roles. God help those men and women who have the audacity to violate God's eternal Word by compromising and doing things their way instead of God's way.

Soli Deo Gloria! — To God alone be the glory!

# END NOTES

1  John MacArthur, Jr. *Rediscovering Pastoral Ministry,* Dallas, Word, 1995, p. 311.

2  Ibid., p. .370.

3  Weldon Crossland. *Better Leaders for Your Church,* New York, Abingdon Press, 1948, p. 33.

4  William Henley's poem: *Invictus*

5  MacArthur, *Ministry,* p. 371.

6  Nolan Harmon, p. 59.

7  Ibid., p.63.

8  Ibid., p. 64.

9  Drs. Eugene Kennedy and Sara Charles, *On Becoming Counselor,* New York, The Crossroad Publishing Company, 1997, p. 400.

10 James D. Murch, *Christian Minister's Manual* Cincinnati, Standard Publishing, 1948, 27–28.

11 Ibid., 16–17.

12 Harwood Pattison, *Making of the Sermon,* American Baptist Publication Society, 1941, p. 3.

13 Murch, *Minister's Manual* p.107–108.

14 MacArthur, *Ministry,* p. 81.

15 Dr. Andrew Blackwood, *Pastoral Leadership*, Nashville, Abingdon Press, 1954, pgs. 6568.

16 Harmon, *Ethics*, p. 198.

17 Blackwood, *Pastoral Leadership*, p. 83.

18 Merrill Tenney, *Zondervan Pictorial Dictionary*, Nashville, Zondervan Publications, 1975, p 637.

# BIBLIOGRAPHY

Blackwood, Andrew T. *Pastoral Leadership.* Abingdon Press: Nashville, 1976.

Boyce, Edward H. *With Christ in the Mount.* Exposition Press: New York, 1951.

Cambron, Mark G. *Bible Doctrines.* Zondervan Publishing: Grand Rapids, 1954.

Crossland, Weldon. *Better Leadership for Your Church.* Abingdon Press: Nashville, 1948.

Cruden, Alexander. *Cruden's Complete Concordance.* Universal Book and Bible House: Philadelphia, 1974.

Davis, Ozora S. *Preaching on Church and Community Occasions.* University of Chicago Press: Chicago, 1942.

Earle, Ralph R. *Adam Clarke Commentary on the Holy Bible.* Baker Book House: Grand Rapids, 1967.

Funk And Wagnall. *Standard Home Reference Dictionary,* Universal Educational Guild: New York City, 1927.

Harkness, Georgia. *Christian Ethics.* Abingdon Press: Nashville, 1946.

Hannon, Nolan B. *Ministerial Ethics and Etiquette.* Abingdon Press: Nashville, MCMXXVIII.

Henle William E. *Invictus.* The New England Encyclopaedia Britannica, First Edition 1768.

Hiscox, Edward T. *The Star Book for Ministers.* The Judson Press: Valley Forge 1878 and 1906.

Jordan, L.G. *The Baptist Standard Directory end Busy Pastor's Guide.* Sunday School Pub. Board of the National Baptist Convention, USA: Nashville, 1929.

Kennedy, Eugene and Sara Charles C., M.D. *On Becoming a Counselor.* The Crossroad Publishing Company: New York, 1990.

MacArthur, John, Jr. *Rediscovering Pastoral Ministry.* Word Publishing: Waco, 1995.

Murch, James, D. *Christian Minister's Manual.* Standard Publishing: Cincinnati, MCMXXXVII.

Pattison, Harwood, T. *The Making of the Sermon.* The American Baptist Publication Society: Chicago, 1941.

Ridgeway, E.F. *Calls to Service.* Longmans Green and Company: London, 1936.

Shoemaker, S.M. Jr. *Twice-Born Ministers.* Fleming H. Revell Co.: London, 1935.

Tenney, Merrill. *Zondervan Pictorial Dictionary.* Zondervan Publication: Nashville, 1975.